AFTER BEAUTIFUL
PATIENCE

ELIAS MALIK

Author's Note

*In the name of Allah, the Most Gracious,
the Most Merciful.*

Life is full of challenges and moments of hardship. This book, "After Beautiful Patience", is a collection of short poems, reminders and verses from the Quran and Hadith, intended to provide hope and comfort.They are meant to uplift, inspire and strengthen your faith, showing that patience in those moments of difficulty leads to great rewards. May these words bring you peace and remind you of the beauty that follows patience. Remember, every dark phase is temporary, and with faith and trust in Allahs plans, light will always find its way through.

"So be patient with a beautiful patience."
(Quran 70:5)

This dunya was not created
for us to find absolute bliss in it.
This dunya will always break us,
cause us pain and sorrow.
But still, we chase after it
and forget what the actual goal is.

"But you prefer the life of this world
even though the Hereafter is far better and more lasting."
(87:16-17)

When your life becomes chaotic,
and the burden on your shoulders feels heavy,
and everything seems too much,
think of Allah and find peace.

"Surely in the remembrance of Allah do hearts find comfort."
(13:28)

Our Ummah is deeply divided by national pride and patriotism. We are too busy looking for differences, forgetting our similarities and what unites us: our religion. Where you come from is absolutely irrelevant. What are you proud of? The true purpose of these differences is to give us the opportunity to get to know and understand each other. Instead of separating us, they should bring us closer together, helping us to appreciate our diversity and strengthen the unity within our community.

"...and made you into peoples and tribes so that you may 'get to' know one another."
(49:13)

"All mankind is from Adam and Eve, an Arab has no superiority over a non-Arab nor a non-Arab has any superiority over an Arab; also a White has no superiority over a Black nor a Black has any superiority over a White except by piety and good action. Learn that every Muslim is a brother to every Muslim and that the Muslims constitute one brotherhood."

- Prophet Muhammad (peace be upon him) in his last sermon

After Beautiful Patience

I spoke with Allah about you.

- *Love Language*

Forget them,
all those who have left,
you will stand before Allah alone.

"And you have certainly come to Us alone as We created you the first time, and you have left whatever We bestowed upon you behind you…"
(6:94)

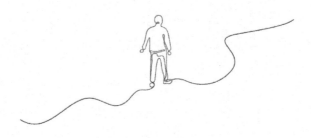

After Beautiful Patience

When someone wrongs you, you have two choices:

Option One:
Seek revenge and risk destroying yourself in the process.

Option Two:
Forgive and Allah will reward you for it.

"Treat people like they treat you."

– no. Treat them better. Be kind. Islam teaches us to respond with kindness. How people behave, act, and treat you shows their character, not yours. Don't let them bring you down to their level.

The Quran encourages us to respond to negativity with positivity: "Good and evil cannot be equal. Respond 'to evil' with what is best, then the one you are in a feud with will be like a close friend." (41:34)

"Forgive him who wrongs you; join him who cuts you off; do good to him who does evil to you, and speak the truth even if it be against yourself."

- Prophet Muhammad (peace be upon him)

Having Iman does not mean that life is free of difficulties. Despite their strong faith, the lives of the prophets were filled with challenges. Prophet Ibrahim was tested with the command to sacrifice his beloved son. Prophet Musa faced the tyranny of Pharaoh and led his people through the desert. Prophet Yusuf was betrayed by his brothers and imprisoned unjustly. Even Prophet Muhammad (peace be upon him) endured persecution and hardship in spreading the message of Islam.

It is certain that we will be tested. Iman means remaining steadfast and patient, even when life gets tough and difficulties arise. True faith is shown in how we handle these trials, trusting in Allah's wisdom and maintaining our believe despite the hardships we face.

"And We will surely test you with something of fear and hunger and a loss of wealth and lives and fruits, but give good tidings to the patient, who, when disaster strikes them, say, 'Indeed we belong to Allah, and indeed to Him we will return.' Those are the ones upon whom are blessings from their Lord and mercy. And it is those who are the [rightly] guided."
(2:155-157)

Do people think once they say, "We believe," that they
will be left without being put to the test?
(29:2)

After Beautiful Patience

She knows she has a pure heart,
and Allah knows it.
That is enough for her.

I pray that
Allah gives you a thousand reasons to laugh
and makes you forget all the pain.
I pray that
the next tears you shed will be tears of joy.
I pray that
you live a life full of joy
as you always wanted.
I pray that
you find a way to forgive all the people
who wronged you.

Amin.

After Beautiful Patience

We never meet by chance;
each soul we encounter
crosses our path with purpose.
They are either a test
or a blessing,
guiding our steps,
shaping our journey,
and helping us grow.

*"And We have made some of you [people] as trial for
others - will you have patience?"*
(25:20)

My dua
always includes your name.

Some people become "more religious" but all you notice is that they become harsher, more judgmental, and arrogant. Its almost like you can see in their eyes that they feel superior. Are you truly feeling that your connection to Allah has become stronger, or are you feeding your ego and elevating yourself above others?

"He who has in his heart the weight of a mustard seed of arrogance shall not enter Paradise." A man asked, "What about a person who likes to wear beautiful clothes and shoes?" The Prophet replied, "Indeed, Allah is beautiful and loves beauty. Arrogance is to reject the truth and look down on people."

- Prophet Muhammad (peace be upon him)

I find it beautiful that in our religion you are judged by your intentions and your effort, not by the outcome. If you do everything with pure intentions and a good heart, be certain Allah will reward you for it.

"Actions are judged by intentions, and every person will be rewarded according to their intention. Thus, he whose migration is for Allah and His Messenger, his migration is for Allah and His Messenger; and he whose migration is to achieve some worldly benefit or to take some woman in marriage, his migration is for that for which he migrated."

- Prophet Muhammad (peace be upon him)

"Be kind, for whenever kindness becomes part of something, it beautifies it."

- Prophet Muhammad (peace be upon him)

One day,
maybe one day,
Allah will reunite us again.
I pray that this time,
it will be forever.

We should be more careful about how we speak. Often, we do not realize the power of language. We say words that are hurtful, worthless, and vulgar. This is why silence is considered a virtue in our religion.

"Whoever believes in Allah and the Last Day should speak a good word or remain silent."

- Prophet Muhammad (peace be upon him)

What is meant for you
will find you.

- Qadr

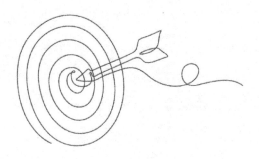

Some people simply shine with Noor,
on their face
and around them.
You immediately feel better
when they are near you.
May Allah surround us with such people
who have a positive influence on us,
and remove those from our lives
who do not benefit us or bring us down.
May He grant us the wisdom
to recognize the difference.

- Noor

I pray to Allah
that you are my destiny.

- *A declaration of love in nine words*

Sometimes you hurt but don't know where and why it hurts. You just know it does. You feel like nobody will understand. You can't even blame them because you can't grasp it yourself. But Allah knows. He made your heart. He understands your pain even when nobody else would. Turn to Him, for He is always there to comfort you and heal your wounds.

"Whether you speak secretly or openly - He certainly knows what is in the heart.
How could He not know His own creation? For He is the Most Subtle, All-Aware."
(67:13-14)

If the pain becomes overwhelming
and you feel like you can't go on anymore,
remember this:

"Allah does not burden a soul beyond that it can bear."
(2:286)

You are stronger than you think,
and Allah is always with you.

Be realistic in all aspects of your life,
except when it comes to your prayers.
Ask Allah for what seems impossible,
for nothing is beyond His power.
Remember, when Allah wills something to happen,
He simply says "Be" and it is.
So, let your duas be boundless,
trusting that Allah can make the unimaginable a reality.

I would rather have a small Nikah with my closest family and friends in the masjid, people I know genuinely wish me well, than an extravagant, lavish wedding.

There is blessing in simplicity.

After Beautiful Patience

Ya Allah,
protect my heart
from getting attached to something
that will not remain.

Here, I find peace and clarity.
The conversations between me and Allah,
when I sit quietly on my prayer mat,
are when I feel most understood.
In those moments,
when the world around me is still,
I open my heart and find comfort.
In the depths of my prayer, I feel a deep connection,
one that gives me strength and hope.
It is during these silent exchanges
that I share my deepest thoughts and worries,
and I feel that Allah hears and understands me.
In these moments,
I truly find peace and clarity.

"Those who have believed and whose hearts are assured by the remembrance of Allah. Unquestionably, by the remembrance of Allah hearts are assured."
(13:28)

A man asked the Prophet about the Hour (Day of Judgment) saying, "When will the Hour be?" The Prophet said, "What have you prepared for it?" The man said, "Nothing, except that I love Allah and His Messenger." The Prophet said, "You will be with those whom you love."

After Beautiful Patience

Ya Allah,
I fell in love with one of Your servants.
Please bless this love,
and make it a source of goodness and strength.
Guide us to love each other for Your sake,
and let our love bring us closer to You.

If it is written for us to be together,
make our union blessed and filled with Your mercy.
If it is not meant to be,
grant me patience and understanding,
and help me trust in Your wisdom and plan for me.

Ameen.

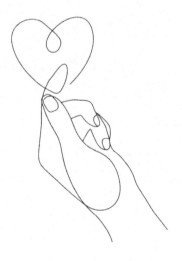

Never think that Allah cannot forgive you,
do not despair over your past.
If you cannot turn to Allah,
who else can you seek refuge with?
He is the All-Forgiving,
the Accepter of Repentance.

"Say, 'O My servants who have transgressed against themselves [by sinning], do not despair of the mercy of Allah. Indeed, Allah forgives all sins. Indeed, it is He who is the Forgiving, the Merciful."
(39:53)

Begin to change your perspective on things and show gratitude.

Your parents "annoy" you?
Alhamdulillah, they are still alive.

You're stressed from school, university, or work?
Alhamdulillah, you have the opportunity for education and earning money.

You don't have money to eat outside?
Alhamdulillah, you have food at home.

You're sick?
Alhamdulillah, your sins are being forgiven.

We must understand that there are people who dream of living our lives. We must stop taking things, whether big or small, for granted. They are not.

"If you are grateful, I will certainly give you more."
(14:7)

Write down the things you are grateful for. Come back every time you find something new. Notice how blessed you are.

"If you tried to count Allah's blessings, you would never be able to number them. Surely Allah is All-Forgiving, Most Merciful."
(16:18)

After Beautiful Patience

If you've left it to Allah,
why are you still worrying?

Now I see everything clearly,
the path I have to take.
May Allah make it easy for me.

- Sirat al-Mustaqim

*"Guide us along the Straight Path,
the Path of those You have blessed—not those You are
displeased with, or those who are astray."
(1:6-7)*

After Beautiful Patience

Everything is written,
and I hope,
that your name
is next to mine.

- *Nasip*

Travel the world,
see the beauty of Allah's creation.
Experience the diversity of landscapes,
the richness of cultures.

Reflect on the One who made all of this.

"Travel through the land and observe how He began creation."
(29:20)

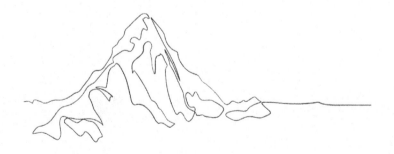

Some people unintentionally push others away from Islam. Instead of giving true nasiha, they speak judgmentally and think harshly. Before you correct someone, ask yourself if it is actually going to benefit them. In Islam, giving advice should be done with kindness and wisdom. The Prophet Muhammad (peace be upon him) said, *"Make things easy and do not make things difficult, give glad tidings and do not cause aversion."* Always ensure that your words are beneficial, and remember that your intention should be to guide and help, not to judge or criticize.

*"What is the world to me? What am I to the world?
Verily, the parable of myself and this world is that of a
rider who seeks shade under a tree, then he moves on and
leaves it behind."*

- Prophet Muhammad (peace be upon him)

After Beautiful Patience

I've done all I can.
Now everything left to say is:

Fi amanillah
I leave you in the care of Allah.

After Beautiful Patience

I will never understand
how one can think
that all of this is random,
in light of the wonders of this world.
To believe that it all has no meaning.
Every detail in nature,
every nuance of life,
is a sign.

" And one of His signs is that He created for you spouses
from among yourselves so that you may find comfort in
them. And He has placed between you compassion and
mercy. Surely in this are signs for people who reflect.
And one of His signs is the creation of the heavens and
the earth and the diversity of your languages and colors.
Surely in this are signs for those of sound knowledge.
And one of His signs is your sleep by night and by day
and your seeking of His bounty. Surely in this are signs
for people who listen.
And one of His signs is that He shows you lightning,
inspiring you with hope and fear. And He sends down
rain from the sky, reviving the earth after its death. Surely
in this are signs for people who understand."
(30:21-24)

"Do you think that We had created you for no reason,
and that you would never be returned to Us?"
(23:115)

The moment
when you realize
that Allah protected your heart
from what it once desired.

"But perhaps you hate a thing and it is good for you; and perhaps you love a thing and it is bad for you. And Allah Knows, while you know not."
(2:216)

You have something so powerful
that it can even change destiny.
Use it.

- Dua

"Nothing can change the Divine decree except dua."

- Prophet Muhammad (peace be upon him)

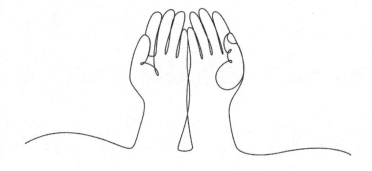

After Beautiful Patience

You can keep worrying about it,
or you can make dua
and put your trust in Allah.
One changes nothing,
and the other changes everything.

After Beautiful Patience

After all this, there will be a day
when you look back and say:

Ya Allah,
this is more than I prayed for.

Help a random stranger. Spread goodness and kindness. Smile as much as you can. Be the reason people believe in good hearts. Nowadays, everything is filled with negativity; a simple smile or compliment can brighten someone's day. Islam teaches us to be a source of light, to show compassion, and to spread positivity wherever we go. Let your actions inspire others and be the goodness you wish to see in the world.

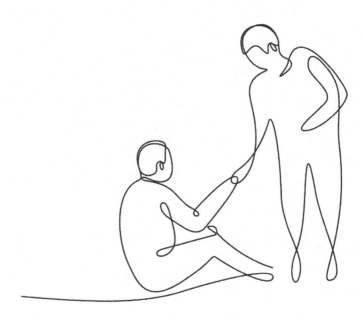

Paradise will be full of sinners
who have repented.
So ask Allah for forgiveness,
for He is Al-Ghaffar,
the Most Merciful,
the All-Forgiving.

"But those who committed evil deeds and then repented
after them and believed - indeed, your Lord, thereafter, is
Forgiving and Merciful."
(7:153)

"And who forgives sins except Allah?"
(3:135)

"When Allah decreed the Creation He pledged Himself by writing in His book which is laid down with Him: 'My mercy prevails over My anger.'"

After Beautiful Patience

When I look into the sky,
I think about the beauty in this world,
then I think how beautiful Jannah must be,
a place with:

Rivers of milk and honey,
Gardens of unparalleled beauty,
Eternal peace and joy,
Reunions with loved ones,

Surely, the beauty of this world is but a glimpse of the wonders that await in Jannah. I pray that Allah makes us among those who will see it.

"Allah has promised the believing men and women gardens under which rivers flow, to stay there forever, and splendid homes in the Gardens of Eternity. And Allah's pleasure is even greater. That is the ultimate triumph."
(9:72)

After Beautiful Patience

I don't know
what I saw in them.
Thank you, Allah,
for clearing my vision again.

After Beautiful Patience

The thought
that your name
has always been next to mine.
You were my destiny.
From the very beginning.

You have a business idea?
Keep it to yourself.

You have achieved your goals?
Keep it to yourself.

You plan to travel?
Keep it to yourself.

You passed an exam?
Keep it to yourself.

You don't need to let everyone know what you're doing and what's happening in your life. Keep it private. Envy and jealousy can ruin the blessings Allah has given you.

The Prophet Muhammad (peace be upon him) warned us: "Be discreet in what you wish to achieve, for verily every blessing has its envier."

Rely on nothing
except Allah alone.

No matter what you have done,
how much you have sinned,
it is never too late
to return to Allah.

The Prophet Muhammad (peace be upon him) said:
"Every son of Adam sins, and the best of those who sin
are those who repent."

Allah says in a Hadith Qudsi:
"O son of Adam, so long as you call upon Me and ask of
Me, I shall forgive you for what you have done, and I
shall not mind. O son of Adam, were your sins to reach
the clouds of the sky and were you then to ask forgiveness
of Me, I would forgive you. O son of Adam, were you to
come to Me with sins nearly as great as the earth and
were you then to face Me, ascribing no partner to Me, I
would bring you forgiveness nearly as great as it."

If the world was blind,
how many people would you impress
with your character?
In Islam, it's the purity of your heart
and the sincerity of your actions
that matter most.

Prophet Muhammad (peace be upon him) said:
"Verily, Allah does not look at your appearance or
wealth, but rather He looks at your hearts and actions."

After Beautiful Patience

Isn't it strange,
everyone wants to be successful,
but only a few
follow the call to success.

Come to prayer,
come to success.

After Beautiful Patience

It took me some time
to realize
that you are the happiness
I prayed for.

After Beautiful Patience

Seems like you forgot,
when everybody left you,
you had nowhere to go,
and life felt overwhelming,
Allah was there
and gave you comfort.

May Allah let you never forget that.

Prophet Muhammad (peace be upon him) said:
"Be mindful of Allah, and you will find Him in front of
you. Get to know Allah in prosperity, and He will know
you in adversity. Know that what has passed you by was
not going to befall you, and what has befallen you was
not going to pass you by. And know that victory comes
with patience, relief with affliction, and ease with
hardship."

Ya Allah,
let me leave this earth
only when You are pleased with me.

Will you wait for her?
"Yes."

How long?
"Until Allah wants us to meet."

If you truly love someone,
then make dua for them.
Again and again,
even when they are not present.

Prophet Muhammad (peace be upon him) said:
"No supplication is more readily answered than the
supplication for someone who is absent."

Private life.
Close circle.
Strong faith.
Five prayers.
Trust in His plan.

Goals

They say Islam is misogynistic.

But our Prophet says:
"The best among you is the one who treats his wife the best."

They say Islam glorifies violence.
But the Quran teaches us:
"...if anyone kills a person – unless in retribution for murder or spreading corruption in the land – it is as if they have killed all of humanity; and if anyone saves a life, it is as if they have saved all of humanity." (5:32)

They say Islam is intolerant of other religions.
But the Quran states:
"For you is your religion, and for me is my religion." (109:6)

They say Islam is backward and against modernization.
But they forget that many significant inventions came from Muslims and that Muslims were pioneers in science in the past.

Islam is perfect. People are not. So do not confuse the actions of someone who calls themselves a Muslim with the teachings of Islam.

When you make dua, be certain that Allah will answer you. The answer may be different from what you expect because He knows what is best for you. Never think that just because things are not happening as you wish, your dua has gone unnoticed. Allah hears every prayer and responds in the most beneficial way. Sometimes the answer is delayed, sometimes it comes in a form we didn't anticipate, and sometimes it's a gentle protection from something harmful we cannot see. Trust in His wisdom and timing, for Allah's plans are always perfect and filled with mercy. Keep your faith strong, and know that every dua is valued and every sincere prayer is answered, even if the response is beyond our immediate understanding. Just as a seed eventually blossoms, your dua too will bear fruit in the way that is best for you.

"Call upon Me; I will respond to you."
(40:60)

It is never luck or chance.
It is always Allah.

After Beautiful Patience

There is something poetic
when Allah protects you
from something you desperately wanted.

How many hearts have you broken?
How do you plan to ever repair them?

Ibn Taymiyyah said:
"Whoever breaks someone's heart is obligated to heal that person's heart."

May Allah surround us with people
who are good for us,
mentally and spiritually;
those who nourish our soul
and constantly remind us of Allah.

Amin.

After Beautiful Patience

Who was there when everyone left?

"Allah"

Forgive them,
as you wish
Allah to forgive you.

Don't highlight the sins and shortcomings of others in public. Instead, cover them and address issues privately. In Islam, maintaining the dignity and honor of others is very important. By concealing the faults of your brothers and sisters, you protect their reputation and earn Allah's favor. The Prophet Muhammad (peace be upon him) said: "Whoever conceals the faults of a Muslim, Allah will conceal his faults in this world and the Hereafter." Show compassion and understanding, and remember that we all have our own imperfections. Approach others with kindness and offer sincere advice in a private and respectful manner, with the intention to uplift and support them rather than bring them down.

If people talk about you,
spread lies and rumors,
remember: reputation among people
holds no true worth.

"Their words should not grieve you. Indeed, all power belongs to Allah. He is the All-Hearing, the All-Knowing."
(10:65)

After Beautiful Patience

Everyone is a slave to something,
Be it money,
status, jobs,
desires, or societal expectations.

As Muslims, we only submit to our creator Allah,
the One who truly deserves our submission.

And the example of those who donate their wealth, seeking Allah's pleasure and believing the reward is certain,1 is that of a garden on a fertile hill: when heavy rain falls, it yields up twice its normal produce. If no heavy rain falls, a drizzle is sufficient. And Allah is All-Seeing of what you do.
(2:265)

Don't trade your akhira
for this dunya.
What are a few decades
compared to eternity?

Once upon a time, there was an old Muslim fisherman, known for his wisdom and contentment. One day, his fishing boat was destroyed in a storm. The villagers came to him and said, "How unfortunate that your boat was destroyed! You have lost your source of income."

The fisherman simply replied, "Alhamdulillah." The villagers criticized him for being detached from reality and naive. A few days later, the fisherman's son found a large pearl in one of the caught fish. The villagers came again and said, "How lucky that your son found this pearl! You will now have more income."

The fisherman again replied simply, "Alhamdulillah." The villagers criticized him once more, this time for not appreciating the value of good fortune. A few weeks later, the fisherman's son tried to sell the pearl and was robbed and injured in the process. Again, the villagers came to the fisherman and said, "How unfortunate that your son was robbed! He will no longer be able to help you with fishing." The fisherman again replied, "Alhamdulillah." The villagers criticized him once more, accusing him of being too passive towards injustices. A few months later, the village was raided by bandits, and all able-bodied men were taken as prisoners. The fisherman's son was spared from captivity due to his previous injury. The villagers came to the fisherman and said, "How lucky that your son was not taken as a prisoner!" The fisherman simply replied, "Alhamdulillah."

"Few of My servants are truly grateful."
(34:13)

A mirage in the desert, from a distance, appears as a beautiful, shimmering oasis, promising water and relief from the heat. However, as you get closer, you realize it's just an illusion created by the refraction of light on the hot sand, offering nothing but more barren desert. The same can be said for this dunya. It may seem attractive and fulfilling from afar, but its true nature is deceptive, holding nothing of real, lasting value compared to the Hereafter.

"Know that the life of this world is but amusement and diversion and adornment and boasting to one another and competition in increase of wealth and children. Like the example of a rain whose [resulting] plant growth pleases the tillers; then it dries and you see it turned yellow; then it becomes [scattered] debris. And in the Hereafter is severe punishment and forgiveness from Allah and approval. And what is the worldly life except the enjoyment of delusion."
(57:20)

After Beautiful Patience

There are people
who suffer in silence.
They smile on the outside,
But bleeding on the inside.
and share their sorrows and grief
only with Allah.

"I only complain of my suffering and my grief to Allah"
(12:86)

Soon everything will make sense.
Just have a little more patience.
Allah will soon show you
why everything had to happen the way it did.

Fiha Khair
There is goodness in every Situation

Whenever it rains,
I say your name,
In every drop that falls,
I whisper a prayer for you.

*The Prophet Muhammad (peace be upon him) said:
"Two are the supplications that are never returned: the
supplication made when the prayer is being called, and
at the time of rainfall."*

Your smile can be a source of hope for someone else.

So smile.
It is Sunnah.

Our heart is the core of our being, yet it is constantly subjected to fluctuations. It is comparable to a leaf dancing unpredictably in the wind, sometimes blowing in one direction, sometimes in another. In this context, Prophet Muhammad (peace be upon him) often repeated this prayer for steadfastness:

"O Turner of the hearts! Make my heart steadfast in Your religion!"

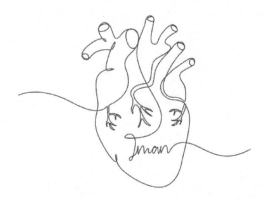

After Beautiful Patience

Hold on to your Iman,
no matter what happens,
it will give you clarity and confidence
in every situation.

It is a largely lost art to speak well, be educated, have good manners, hold values and beliefs, and carry yourself with grace and class. Being this way will set you apart from most people today, even if others do not appreciate it – you will.

A simple rhetorical question from the Quran,
and you rethink your entire life.

"So where are you going?"
(81:26)

Blessed are the strangers.

Sometimes we do or don't do certain things regarding our religion because of the reaction of others. We think, "Maybe they will think differently of me." I fell victim to that myself until I asked myself: "Am I trying to please the Creator or His creation? What is more important?"
I realized that pleasing Allah is what truly matters. I shouldn't be afraid to be strange or an outcast if it means practicing my religion. If staying true to my faith sets me apart, so be it. Allah's approval is what counts the most.

The Prophet Muhammad (peace be upon him) said:
"Islam began as something strange and will return to being strange, so blessed are the strangers."

Do good and let go of expectations and the desire for recognition. Your reward will not come from people.

"(The righteous) give food to the poor, the orphan, and the captive, for the love of Allah. They say, 'We feed you only for the sake of Allah; we do not want any reward or thanks from you.'"
(76:8-9)

An Arabic proverb: Do good and throw it into the sea.

Keep your word always,
don't take promises lightly.
Every promise is a reflection of your integrity.

Honor your word.

The Prophet Muhammad (peace be upon him) said:
"The signs of a hypocrite are three: Whenever he speaks,
he tells a lie; whenever he promises, he breaks it; and if
he is trusted, he betrays his trust."

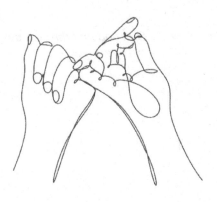

Pray.

I promise you, it will change your life. In Islam, prayer is essential. It is a direct connection with Allah and a source of immense peace and strength.

Make each prayer sincere. Feel the peace and guidance from regular prayer.

"When you have finished the prayer, remember Allah—standing, sitting, and lying down. But when you are secure, re-establish 'regular' prayer. Surely prayer is an obligation at specific times for the believers."
(4:103)

"She believed in me when people rejected me."

Prophet Muhammad (peace be upon him) about his wife Khadijah

After Beautiful Patience

No tear falls
that Allah does not notice.

Allah will soon reward your pain.

If you have a good heart
and are kind,
thank Allah.
In a generation where it's become cool
to show no feelings
and to treat people poorly,
be different,
be sincere.
Good deeds are never in vain.

"Indeed, the best among you are those who have the best character!"

- Prophet Muhammad (peace be upon him)

Even if the whole world turns against you,
if you have Allah,
you have nothing to fear.

Those who were warned, "Your enemies have mobilized their forces against you, so fear them," the warning only made them grow stronger in faith and they replied, "Allah ˹alone˺ is sufficient ˹as an aid˺ for us and ˹He˺ is the best Protector."
(3:173)

How often we forget
that angels sit on our shoulders
and write.
Write, write, write…

After Beautiful Patience

Ya Allah,
I asked You
to remove people
that don't wish well for me,
and I started losing friends.

So I pray
that You replace them
with people
whose hearts are connected to You.

But if none are destined for me,
I ask You
to be my only friend.

Ameen.

Don't overthink.
It's simple.

*"Once you make a decision, put your trust in Allah.
Surely, Allah loves those who trust in Him."
(3.159)*

When the wife of Imam Ahmad Ibn Hanbal passed away, he said the following words: "By Allah, I lived with my wife for 40 years and we never had a dispute." He was asked: How? He said: "Whenever she was angry and wanted to argue, I remained quiet. And whenever I was angry and wanted to argue, she remained quiet."

O Allah, You who are the Protector and Guardian, protect my mother as she protected me when I was little. Fill her life with happiness and joy, and make her one of the happiest among Your creations. Grant her health, contentment, and a heart full of peace.

How easily one can explain to someone why they should
do good:

"Is there any reward for goodness except goodness?"
(55:60)

She is the girl
who appears strong on the outside,
yet is breaking inside.
She is the one who is there for everyone,
yet no one is there for her,
except Allah.
So she turns her tears into prayers,
knowing He will never abandon her.

"And among His signs is this, that He created for you mates from among yourselves that you may find tranquility in them, and He placed between you affection and mercy. Indeed, in that are signs for people who reflect."
(30:21)

I have forgiven you,
not because you deserved it,
but because otherwise,
Allah would bring us face to face once more.

But I never want to see you again.

"Indeed, the righteous will be among gardens and springs, accepting what their Lord has given them. Indeed, they were before that doers of good. They used to sleep but little of the night, and in the hours before dawn they would ask forgiveness."
(51:15-18)

Life hurts,
but we survive
with prayer
and our faith.

After Beautiful Patience

The reward
for patience
is always sweet.

Pain that brings you closer to Allah
is better than joy that distances you from Him.

You've changed for the better,
and not everyone will understand.
But they don't need to.
You are trying to please Allah,
not them.

Alhamdulillah

You've
Changed

Once, during a military expedition, the wife of the Prophet Muhammad (peace be upon him), Aisha (r.a.), lost her necklace. Despite being in the middle of a campaign and surrounded by enemies, the Prophet ordered the entire army to stop and search for it. He didn't tell her to get a new one, nor did Aisha (r.a.) demand that he stop and search for it. That's true love. True love means caring deeply for your loved ones and putting their needs first.

My parents,
are everything I have.
I will always be there for them.
I will make them proud and happy one day,
Inshallah.

"And your Lord has decreed that you worship none but Him, and that you be kind to your parents. Whether one or both of them attain old age in your life, say not to them a word of disrespect, nor repel them, but address them in terms of honor. And lower to them the wing of humility out of mercy, and say: 'My Lord, have mercy upon them as they brought me up when I was small.'"
(17:23-24)

The Repentance of Abu Nuwas

Let me tell you the story of Abu Nuwas, a famous poet known for his indulgence in alcohol and obscene expressions. His fame reached its peak when he publicly recited vulgar verses and sang offensive songs. But then, he underwent a profound transformation and made Tauba. People were astonished – Abu Nuwas, the notorious drinker? The indecent man? It seemed almost unbelievable that Allah would forgive him and show him mercy.

However, Abu Nuwas continued to write poetry. Under his deathbed, verses were found that, according to his wife, were the last he ever wrote. They read:

"O my Lord, if the greatness of my sins increase, then I know that Your forgiveness is greaterIf only the righteous called on You, then who would the criminal go to?I call on You my Lord, as you commanded, with reverence And if You turn my hands away, then who else will have mercy?"

After Beautiful Patience

Ya Allah,
turn every tear
my mother has shed because of me
into a river for her in Paradise.

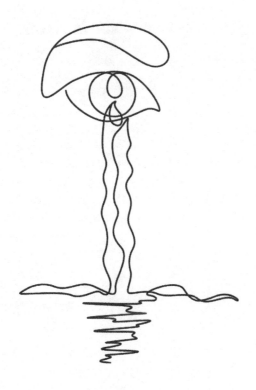

After Beautiful Patience

Ya Allah,
I trust Your plans
more than my own.
Even if nothing makes sense to me right now,
I know that You will protect me
and lead me to the best possible outcome.
Until then, let me not lose hope
and help me to maintain patience.

"And Satan will say when the matter has been concluded, 'Indeed, Allah had promised you the promise of truth. And I promised you, but I betrayed you. But I had no authority over you except that I invited you, and you responded to me. So do not blame me; but blame yourselves. I cannot be called to your aid, nor can you be called to my aid. Indeed, I deny your association of me [with Allah] before. Indeed, for the wrongdoers is a painful punishment."
(14:22)

Every time I read this aya, I get chills all over my body. It is a reminder that we can blame nobody but ourselves for our shortcomings. Shaytan had no power over us; he just invited us to sin, and we chose to respond. We are the ones responsible for our actions and decisions.

There is so much peace in leaving things to Allah. We stress so much in our daily lives: "How will I pay my bills? How can I make more money?" But if we trust that Allah is Al-Razzaq - the Provider - we would find comfort and reassurance in His care.

The Prophet Muhammad (peace be upon him) said:
"If you were to rely upon Allah with the reliance He is due, you would be given provision like the birds. They go out hungry in the morning and return with full bellies in the evening."

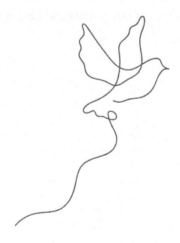

Reflect on how you use your time

Time is something that, once spent, won't come back. But often, we don't fully grasp its value. Be honest with yourself and ask: How do you use your time? Are you worshipping Allah, striving to become a better person, and working on self-improvement? Or are you wasting time on social media, engaging in meaningless conversations and activities that don't benefit you?

1.By time,

2. Indeed, mankind is in loss,

3. Except for those who have believed and done righteous deeds and advised each other to truth and advised each other to patience.

- English translation of Surah Al-Asr (103:1-3)

After Beautiful Patience

When your situation seems hopeless,
remember Allah.

*"And whoever is mindful of Allah, He will make a way
out for them."*
(65:2)

Soulmates in Islam

In Islam, the concept of soulmates is rooted in the idea that souls were created in a realm before this world, and that certain souls were meant to find each other in this life. This profound connection can explain why we feel an instant attraction or deep bond with certain individuals.

The Prophet Muhammad (peace be upon him) spoke about this in a Hadith:

"Souls are like conscripted soldiers; those whom they recognize, they get along with, and those whom they do not recognize, they will not get along with."

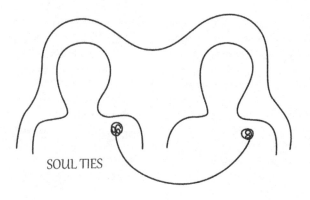

SOUL TIES

After Beautiful Patience

I'm way more interested
in what Allah thinks of me
than random people
I don't know.

As humans, we always want more.
After we achieve one materialistic goal,
we immediately seek the next—
whether it's the newest car, the latest smartphone,
or other trendy possessions.

However, we often fail to understand that these things
cannot fill the void within us.

The Prophet Muhammad (peace be upon him) said:
"If the son of Adam were to possess two valleys of gold,
he would long for a third. But nothing can fill the belly of
the son of Adam except dust. And Allah forgives him who
repents to Him."

After Beautiful Patience

I ask Allah to help me
to love you correctly,
to make sure
you know there will always be someone
who is there for you.

I pray that He lets you know that you are seen and loved.

Till death do us part is not enough.
Fi dunya wa fil akhira,
I wish to be with you in this life and the next.

A love that never dies

"What is wrong with me, standing at the graveside saying salam to the one who has passed. The grave of my lover but she is not responding to my greeting. My lover why are you not responding to my salam?"

- Poem That Hazrat Ali Recited At The Graveside Of Hazrat Fatima

Everybody dies.
Death is what makes us equal. No matter our status,
wealth, or power, we all face the same end.

"Woe to every backbiter, slanderer,
who amasses wealth and keeps on counting it,
thinking that their wealth will make them immortal!
Not at all! They will certainly be thrown into the
Crusher."

- Translations of Surah Al-Humazah (104:1-4)

Maybe you don't need more.

Maybe you just need to appreciate what Allah has already given you. The grass is always greener on the other side, but you need to value what you have.

After Beautiful Patience

I'm in a phase in my life where
I don't really care who wants to leave.
I no longer force relationships.

All I care about is maintaining my connection to Allah.
If someone wants to leave, I let them.

Late Regret:

""Oh! I wish I had followed the Way along with the Messenger!"
(25:27)

"Woe to me! I wish I had never taken so-and-so as a close friend."
(25:28)

"Oh, I wish I had not associated with my Lord anyone."
(18:42)

""Oh! If only we could be sent back, we would never deny the signs of our Lord and we would ˈsurelyˈ be of the believers."
(6:27)

"Oh, how we wish we had obeyed Allah and obeyed the Messenger."
(33:66)

The most beautiful endings
are for those
who are patient.

*"So be patient; indeed, the [best] outcome is for the
righteous."*
(11:49)

After Beautiful Patience

I am so determined to improve.
To pray more.
To be more thankful.
To become kinder.
To speak beautifully.
To be better in every way.

There is always room for improvement.

Unknown to the people,
known by the angels.

Their deeds go unnoticed by the world,
but they are cherished in the heavens.

All this pain,
all the people who hurt you,
yet you didn't complain even a little.
You trusted Him completely.

May Allah make it easy for you.

*"Peace be upon you for what you patiently endured. And
excellent is the final home."*
(13:24)

In case you feel alone, remember:

"He is with you wherever you are."
(57:4)

Dont just thank Allah when things are going right. Thank him even when things are difficult. It's easy to feel thankful when everything is going smoothly, but true faith and strength are shown when we maintain our thankfulness even in tough times. Difficulties often teach us valuable lessons, help us grow, and bring us closer to understanding ourselves and our faith. By thanking Allah during these trials, we acknowledge that there's a purpose and a lesson in every situation, and that His guidance and support are constant, no matter what we're facing. This attitude of continuous gratitude can transform our perspective, helping us to see the light even in the darkest of times.

"And when adversity touches man, he calls upon Us, whether lying on his side or sitting or standing; but when We remove from him his adversity, he continues in disobedience as if he had never called upon Us to remove an adversity that touched him. Thus is made pleasing to the transgressors that which they have been doing."
(10:12)

If you feel far from Allah,
ask yourself:
who moved?

*"And We have already created man and know what his
soul whispers to him, and We are closer to him than [his]
jugular vein."*
(50:16)

Whatever happens tomorrow,
we've had today.

Alhamdulillah

If you cultivate a garden,
you don't dig up the seed every day
to check if the flower is growing.
You just sow, water the plants,
and wait patiently.
The same is true for yourself.
Try to improve every day,
focus on your daily prayers,
and give yourself time.
Aim for long-term change.
Patience is key.

After Beautiful Patience

Allah created the beautiful blue oceans,
the majestic mountains,
and the twinkling stars.
He made the vibrant flowers,
lush forests, and flowing rivers.

Yet, He calls us humans His most beautiful creation.
Subhanallah.

"Indeed, We created humans in the best form."
(95:4)

A Wonderful Story of Human Beauty

Qurtubi, on this occasion, cites a story of Isa Ibn Musa Hashimi. He was a high ranking officer in the royal court of Caliph Abu Ja'far Mansur. The officer loved his wife very much. Once he was sitting with his wife in a moonlit night and suddenly cried out: "You are divorced thrice if you are not more beautiful than the moon." As soon as the wife heard this, she went into seclusion and veiled herself, on the grounds that the husband has pronounced three express divorce on her. It was said in joke. However, the law of express divorce is that it becomes effective whether uttered jokingly or seriously. Isa Ibn Musa spent the night restlessly and in grief. The next morning, he paid a visit to Caliph Abu Ja'far Mansur and recounted to him the whole story. Caliph Abu Ja'far Mansur invited all the jurists of the city and put the case before them. All the jurists unanimously agreed that the divorce has become effective, because no human being can possibly be more beautiful than the moon. There was, however, one scholar, a student of Imam Abu Hanifah who remained silent. Mansur asked him: "Why are you so quiet?" He recited 'Bismillah to the end' and then recited Surah Tin and explained: "Ruler of the Faithful, Allah says that He has created man in the best composition or in the finest mould. Nothing can be more beautiful than man." Having heard this, all the scholars and jurists were perplexed. None of them opposed him. Mansur ordered that the divorce is not effective.

How many times should we forgive a person?

As many times you would like Allah forgive you.

„You seem so strong despite everything you been through. Whats your secret?"

„I trust Allah."

There are people
who have gone through it all –
pain, abandonment, betrayal,
loss –
yet they still choose to spread love.
It's almost as if their hearts
are not capable of hate.

I admire that

In a religion
where even a thorn that pricks you
erases your sins,
imagine how many are forgiven through all the hardships
you've been through.

- A Diffrent Perspective

Prophet Muhammad (peace be upon him) said:
*"No fatigue, nor disease, nor sorrow, nor sadness, nor
hurt, nor distress befalls a Muslim, even if it were the
prick he receives from a thorn, but that Allah expiates
some of his sins for that."*

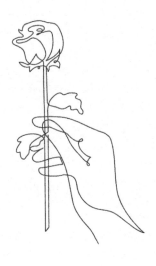

"Strange is the case of the believer, for there is good for him in every matter; this is not the case for anyone but a believer. If joy visits him, he thanks Allah and it is good for him. If trouble befalls him, he shows patience and it is good for him."

- Prophet Muhammad (peace be upon him)

"You must remember Allah, for it is a cure. And you must beware of remembering the people, for indeed it is a sickness."

- Hazrat Umar ibn al-Khattab

After Beautiful Patience

- Slow down

Take a moment to reflect.
You are so caught up
with the hecticness of life:
school, university, work, family.
It stresses you out,
everything goes so fast.
In the chaos of life,
be aware of your surroundings.
Don't forget to take a moment,
breathe deeply,
and look around you.
Appreciate the blessings Allah has given you.
Notice the small joys,
the beauty in everyday moments,
the love of those around you.
Find peace in your heart,
and thank Allah for every blessing.
Slow down, and let gratitude fill your soul.

Dunya called him:
"How can you forget me?"

He replied:
*"I no longer want you.
Jannah is all I desire."*

After Beautiful Patience

Look around you.
All the blessings
your eyes
became blind to see.

"So which of the favors of your Lord would you deny?"
(55:13)

Are you rich?
"Yes, Alhamdulillah."

How much money do you have in the bank?
"Not much. But I have my Faith."

The Prophet Muhammad (peace be upon him) said:
"Wealth is not in having many possessions. Rather, true wealth is the richness of the soul."

Allah brings you
from darkness into light.
How can you stay away from Him?

"Allah is the Protector of those who have faith: from the depths of darkness He will lead them forth into light. Of those who reject faith the patrons are the evil ones: from light they will lead them forth into the depths of darkness. They will be companions of the fire, to dwell therein (forever)."
(2:257)

After Beautiful Patience

Under every smile,
there is an untold story,
things only Allah knows.

Behind each laugh,
there may be hidden pain,
and silent prayers that remain unseen.

May Allah ease every hidden struggle,
and bring comfort to every silent heart.

After Beautiful Patience

Ya Allah, forgive me
for the times I have been ungrateful,
when I took Your blessings for granted,
when I desired more even though I had enough,
when I compared myself to those who have more,
instead of those who have less than me,
and failed to appreciate all that I have.

The Prophet Muhammad (peace be upon him) said:
"Treat women kindly, for a woman is created from a rib,
and the most crooked portion of the rib is its upper
portion. If you try to straighten it, you will break it, and if
you leave it, it will remain crooked. So treat women
kindly."

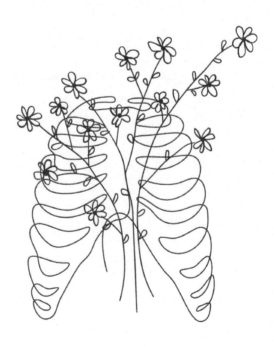

After Beautiful Patience

As I grew older, I realized that not everything people do needs a reaction. Often, it is better to respond with calmness and kindness instead of trying to argue.

"And the servants of the Most Merciful are those who walk upon the earth humbly, and when the ignorant address them [harshly], they respond with peace."
(25:63)

Let go.
Set your heart free.
Holding onto people
that don't want to be in your life
will only hurt.

*"When a thing disturbs the peace of your heart,
give it up."*

- Prophet Muhammad (peace be upon him)

After Beautiful Patience

May Allah bless you with people
who support you,
encourage your growth,
and genuinely care for you -
not for what you provide for them,
but for who you are.

May He bless you with people
who bring you closer to Him,
remind you of Him,
and help strengthen your faith.

*May He surround you with friends who inspire you to be
your best self.*

I thank Allah that He gave me a friend like you. A friend who always has my back, who defends my name when I'm not around, and who wants to see me win. A friend who lifts me up when I'm down, who shares my joys and sorrows, and who encourages me to be my best. I thank Him for blessing me with such a true and loyal friend, and I thank you for being that friend. Your support and kindness mean the world to me.

- *Message to a Friend*

Allah tests those whom He loves. So, whatever you are going through right now, remember that it is a sign of His love and care for you. Stay patient and keep your faith strong.

The Prophet Muhammad (peace be upon him) said:
"Indeed, greater reward comes with greater trial. And indeed, when Allah loves a people, He subjects them to trials. Whoever accepts that, wins His pleasure; but whoever is discontent with that, earns His wrath."

A blessing may come to you because you wished it for someone else.

The Prophet Muhammad (peace be upon him) said:
"None of you truly believes until he loves for his brother what he loves for himself."

The Salaf used to comfort each other upon facing
calamities by saying:

"This life is but a few days and Jannah is the promise...."

Love for the sake of Allah
is one of the greatest acts of worship.
To help others, to be there for them, and to build sincere
bonds.

*The Prophet Muhammad (peace be upon him) said that
among those whom Allah will shade on the Day when
there is no shade but His are two people who love each
other for the sake of Allah, meeting and parting on that
basis.*

What if everything only gets better?
What if it didn't work out
because Allah had something better planned for you?
What if the things you prayed for
are being prepared in ways you can't yet see?

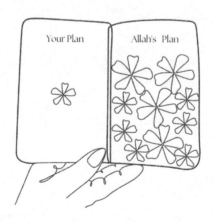

Don't be proud of your reputation. Remember, it is not entirely a reflection of your true self but rather the grace of Allah that veils your faults.

"Know that if people are impressed by you, in reality they are impressed by the beauty of Allah's covering of your sins."

- Ibn al-Jawzi

Hazrat Abu Bakr (r.a.) used to say this dua:

"O Allah, make me better than what they think of me, and forgive me for what they do not know about me, and do not take me to account for what they say about me."

It teaches us to aspire to be better internally than how we are perceived externally. Hazrat Abu Bakr's prayer is a beautiful reminder of the need for constant self-improvement and reliance on Allah's mercy.

That you are like you are
is not the problem.
The problem begins
if you think
"I'm just like that"
and don't try to become better.

Everyone sins,
but not everyone is at war with his sins.

*"Indeed, Allah will not change the condition of a people
until they change what is in themselves."*
(13:11)

Strive for excellence. Eat well, work out, read, and excel academically. Be kind and help others. Pray regularly and be someone who aims for positive change. Remember, most people wont read the Quran to get an impression of islam. they will judge by the people they meet. You are an ambassador of your faith and values - act like it.

Before the prophet left this world he said in his last sermon:

„...Do treat your women well and be kind to them for they are your partners and committed helpers."

After Beautiful Patience

Snow falls from the heaven pure
but as its falls
it becomes soiled by the earth
and if it melts
you can see all the dirt
it inherited.

This is our challenge as believers:
to not allow the dirt and darkness of this dunya
to consume our soul.

- *Snowfall*

Read the Quran
Pray Salah
Go to the Mosque
Listen to the Qutbah
Give Charity
Help others

Decorate your Life
Design your Soul

After Beautiful Patience

In this journey of life,
where the days go by fast
and everything becomes so hectic sometimes,

now and then
take a moment
and remember
what the destination
of this travel is.

*"Every soul will taste death. Then to Us will you be
returned."*
(29:57)

After Beautiful Patience

Some doors might close
because you try to better your relationship with Allah.
But He is Al-Fattah,
the Opener.

He will open doors for you
that you never imagined.

Light attracts moths, and your shine may provoke envy and jealousy in some people. They will try to dim it and throw shade.

Ya Allah, keep such people away from my life and surround me with those who appreciate my light.

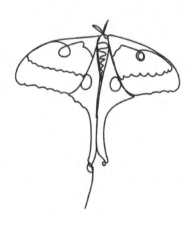

"What if I had done this? What if I had done that? Then this wouldn't have happened..."

Stop overthinking.
It was Allah's plan. So don't lose yourself in the past. Look forward and be patient with whatever Allah has decreed for you.

The Prophet Muhammad (peace be upon him) said: "If something bad befalls you, do not say: 'If only I had done such-and-such, then such-and-such would have happened.' Say: 'Qaddar Allah wa ma sha'a fa'al' (Allah decrees, and what He wills, He does), for (the word) 'if' opens the (door to the) deeds of Satan."

"The supplication of the distressed is this: O Allah, I hope in Your mercy. Do not abandon me to myself, not even for a moment, and take care of all my affairs. There is no God but You."

- Prophet Muhammad (peace be upon him)

In Japan, there is a tradition called Kintsugi in which broken objects are mended with gold, honoring the flaw as a special part of the object's story, enhancing its beauty. Similarly, when we feel broken, we can find comfort in the belief that Allah is the ultimate healer and fixer. Our imperfections and struggles can be seen as opportunities for growth and learning, as Allah mends and strengthens us through our experiences. Just as the golden repairs add value to broken objects, Allah's guidance and support can transform our brokenness into something beautiful, making us stronger and more resilient in the process.

- Embrace the brokenness

*"Allah the Exalted said
: 'I am as My servant expects Me to be. I am with him
when he remembers Me. If he remembers Me in himself, I
remember him in Myself. If he remembers Me in a
gathering, I remember him in a better gathering. If he
draws near to Me a hand's length, I draw near to him an
arm's length. If he comes to Me walking, I go to him
running.'"*

To plant a garden is to believe in the future. It's about hope, faith, and patience, much like our trust in Allah's plan. Just as we nurture seeds with care, we must nurture our faith with prayer, good deeds, and reliance on Allah. By doing so, we prepare for a future filled with His blessings and mercy. Remember, every effort we make today, no matter how small, contributes to a bountiful harvest in this life and the Hereafter. Keep planting good seeds in your heart and actions, for Allah loves those who cultivate goodness and trust in Him.

After Beautiful Patience

Ya Allah,
You are the All-Forgiving,
You love to forgive.
Therefore, I ask You
to forgive me
and to grant me the strength
to forgive,
just as I wish to be forgiven,
and also to forgive the one
who is reading this.

References and Sources

Page 3
Source: Farewell Sermon of Prophet Muhammad (peace be upon him), various hadith collections and historical records.
Classification: Generally accepted as authentic by Islamic scholars
Page 14
Source: Sahih Muslim, Book 1, Hadith 91
Classification: Sahih (Authentic)
Page 15
Source: Sahih al-Bukhari, Book 1, Hadith 1
Classification: Sahih (Authentic)
Page 16
Source: Sahih Muslim, Book 45, Hadith 100 (Hadith 2594 in some collections)
Classification: Sahih (Authentic)
Page 18
Source: Sahih al-Bukhari, Book 78, Hadith 157 (Hadith 6475 in some collections)
Classification: Sahih (Authentic)
Page 28
Source: Sahih al-Bukhari, Book 57, Hadith 37 (Hadith 3688 in some collections)
Classification: Sahih (Authentic)
Page 37
Source: Sahih al-Bukhari, Book 78, Hadith 152; Sahih Muslim, Book 32, Hadith 6
Classification: Sahih (Authentic)
Page 38
Source: Jami' at-Tirmidhi, Vol. 4, Book 10, Hadith 2377
Classification: Sahih (Authentic)
Page 42
Source: Sunan Ibn Majah, Book 34, Hadith 90
Classification: Hasan (Good)
Page 47
Source: Sahih al-Bukhari, Book 93, Hadith 501 (Hadith 3194 in some collections); Sahih Muslim, Book 50, Hadith 13 (Hadith 2751 in some collections)
Classification: Sahih (Authentic)

Page 51
Source: Al-Mu'jam al-Kabir, Hadith 11822
Classification: Hasan (Good)
Page 53
Source: Sunan Ibn Majah, Book 37, Hadith 4251
Classification: Hasan (Good)
Source: Jami' at-Tirmidhi, Vol. 5, Book 42, Hadith 3540
Classification: Hasan (Good)
Page 54
Source: Sahih Muslim, Book 32, Hadith 6220
Classification: Sahih (Authentic)
Page 57
Source: Sunan at-Tirmidhi, Vol. 4, Book 7, Hadith 2516
Classification: Hasan (Good)
Page 60
Source: Sunan Abu Dawood, Book 8, Hadith 1534
Classification: Sahih (Authentic)
Page 62
Source: Sunan at-Tirmidhi, Vol. 1, Book 7, Hadith 1162
Classification: Sahih (Authentic)
Page 66
Majmu ul Fatawa 18/384
Page 70
Source: Sahih Muslim, Book 45, Hadith 89 (Hadith 2580 in some collections)
Classification: Sahih (Authentic)
Page 81
Source: Sunan Abu Dawood, Book 3, Hadith 2535
Classification: Hasan (Good)
Page 83
Source: Jami' at-Tirmidhi, Vol. 5, Book 44, Hadith 3522
Classification: Sahih (Authentic)
Page 87
Source: Sahih Muslim, Book 1, Hadith 270 (also found in Sahih Muslim 145)
Classification: Sahih (Authentic)
Page 89
Source: Sahih al-Bukhari, Book 2, Hadith 33 (Hadith 6095 in some collections)
Sahih Muslim, Book 1, Hadith 112 (Hadith 59 in some collections)
Classification: Sahih (Authentic)

Page 91

Source: Sahih al-Bukhari, Book 58, Hadith 164

Classification: Sahih (Authentic)

Page 93

Source: Sahih al-Bukhari, Book 73, Hadith 56 (Hadith 3559 in some collections)

Sahih Muslim, Book 45, Hadith 68 (Hadith 2321 in some collections)

Classification: Sahih (Authentic)

Page 98

Source: Tarikh Baghdad. 16/626

Page 109

Source: Sahih al-Bukhari, Book 59, Hadith 462

Sahih Muslim, Book 9, Hadith 356

Classification: Sahih (Authentic)

Page 115

Source: Jami' at-Tirmidhi, Vol. 4, Book 10, Hadith 2344

Classification: Hasan (Good)

Page 119

Source: Sahih Muslim, Book 45, Hadith 159 (Hadith 2638 in some collections)

Classification: Sahih (Authentic)

Page 121

Source:

Sahih al-Bukhari, Book 76, Hadith 447

Sahih Muslim, Book 39, Hadith 2429

Classification: Sahih (Authentic)

Page 139

Ma'ariful-Qur'an , Volume 8, page 825

Page 143

Source:Sahih al-Bukhari, Book 70, Hadith 545

Sahih Muslim, Book 45, Hadith 49 (Hadith 2573 in some collections)

Classification: Sahih (Authentic)

Page 144

Source: Sahih Muslim, Book 55, Hadith 64 (Hadith 2999 in some collections)

Classification: Sahih (Authentic)

Paige 145

Kitabuz Zuhd of Imam Ahmad, Hadith: 644, Kitabuz Zuhd of Imam Hannad, Hadith: 1111, Kitabus Samt, Hadith: 204 and 658, Al Ghibah Wan Namimah, Hadith: 67)

Page 149

Source: Sahih al-Bukhari, Book 76, Hadith 453

Sahih Muslim, Book 5, Hadith 2287

Classification: Sahih (Authentic)

Page 153

Source: Sahih al-Bukhari, Book 62, Hadith 114 (Hadith 3331 in some collections)

Sahih Muslim, Book 8, Hadith 3468

Classification: Sahih (Authentic)

Page 155

Source: Sunan Ibn Majah, Vol. 5, Book 37, Hadith 4245

Classification: Hasan (Good)

Page 158

Source: Jami' at-Tirmidhi, Vol. 4, Book 10, Hadith 2396

Classification: Hasan (Good)

Page 159

Source: Sahih al-Bukhari, Book 2, Hadith 13

Sahih Muslim, Book 1, Hadith 45

Classification: Sahih (Authentic)

Page 161

Source: Sahih al-Bukhari, Book 24, Hadith 504

Sahih Muslim, Book 32, Hadith 621 (Hadith 1031 in some collections)

Classification: Sahih (Authentic)

Page 167

Farewell Sermon of Prophet Muhammad (peace be upon him), various hadith collections and historical records.

Page 173

Source: Sahih Muslim, Book 33, Hadith 6441 (Hadith 2664 in some collections)

Classification: Sahih (Authentic)

Page 174

Sunan Abu Dawood, Book 8, Hadith 5090

Al-Adab Al-Mufrad, Hadith 725

Page 176

Source: Sahih al-Bukhari, Book 93, Hadith 502

Sahih Muslim, Book 48, Hadith 19 (Hadith 2675 in some collections)

Classification: Sahih (Authentic)

Afterword

Thank you to everyone who took the time to read these lines.
If you enjoyed them, feel free to share them in your stories,
on social media, and wherever you connect with others.
Please also consider leaving a review on Amazon. As the
Prophet Muhammad (peace be upon him) said: "Whoever
guides someone to goodness will have a reward like one who
did it".
By sharing goodness, you can help others and do something
good yourself. Let's spread positivity together.

If you are interested in Islamic streetwear inspired by the
book, check out **@IMAN.STUDIOS** (imanstudios.eu)

I am grateful that you are a part of this story.

@ELIASMALIKPOETRY

Elias Malik
c/o AutorenServices.de
Birkenallee 24, 36037 Fulda
Title: After Beautiful Patience Author: Elias Malik
ISBN: 99798334704176
First Edition: 2024
Cover Design: Elias Malik

Made in the USA
Monee, IL
21 December 2024

75061124R00111